Sweet!

80 recipes for the most delicious desserts, cakes and coffee snacks

Colophon

Food
Caplan
Editing
Maaike van Helmond
Design
Deesje Laméris, Suzanne Groenewegen
Photography
Food4eyes.com
Assistant publisher
Josje Kets
Publisher
Fridie van Loon

© Visconti

ISBN 978-90-8724-092-9

© English edition: Miller Books 2008
email@miller-books.com
www.miller-books.com

Foreword

Do you fancy something nice when it's time for a cup of coffee or tea? Or do you want a more elaborate brunch on Sunday morning than during the rest of the week? And what about children's parties, something scrumptious will have to be made for those. For all these moments, there is one terrific solution: something Sweet!

There is nothing better than a delicious cake or a refreshing sweet drink. It satisfies your sweet cravings and gives you a wonderful feeling into the bargain. What about apple dumplings with cinnamon for example, caramel pineapple ice-cream, a tartlet with strawberry mousse or brownies with walnuts? Sweet! has the most delicious desserts, cakes and biscuits, from traditional ones to new favourites and for every moment of the day. These recipes are all mouth-watering, even at the preparation stage. So, enjoy... having a sweet tooth is okay!

Please note: The recipes in this book are for four sweet lovers unless otherwise stated.

Contents

Sweeeeeet

Mention confectionery and a smile will involuntarily appear on many people's faces. With good reason, sweet things symbolize pampering, enjoyment and cosiness. A delicious bar of chocolate, a tasty cake or a wonderfully sweet dessert...Just thinking about them makes your mouth water!

Whether you want a snack at teatime or need a finishing touch for an elaborate dinner, Sweet! gives numerous options.
This cookery book contains 80 recipes for the most delicious cakes, biscuits and other sweet things for any moment of the day; from breakfast to dessert, from drinks to chocolate. Children are not forgotten either. In other words, Sweet! is an absolute must in the kitchen of anyone with a sweet tooth!

Pleasant feelings
Sweet is one of the five basic tastes together with salty, sour, bitter and umami (Japanese for spicy). No matter how good all these tastes are; sweet remains a firm favourite. There are various substances that have a sweet taste, but sugar is the one that is most familiar.

In childhood, you learn that sugar can perform miracles. On a rusk, in otherwise sour yogurt and even with apple sauce, everything tastes much better given a sprinkling of sugar. No wonder that sugar evokes pleasant feelings later in life.
This is not just caused by the magic potion called sugar. Even before you became acquainted with the taste of sugar, you experienced the pleasant sensation of sweetness. Mother's milk is sweet and is the very first taste you experience as a baby. In other words, you were hungry, started to cry, drank some of that wonderful, sweet milk and the hunger pangs made way for a very satisfied feeling. No wonder sweetness and that pleasant feeling remain connected for the rest of your life.

Offering
Sugar is more than just a sweetener. It was once used as an offering to bring prosperity and good luck. There are still various festive occasions when this custom can be observed. For example, sweets handed out by bride at a wedding or sugar plums at Christmas.

Men who eat sweets regularly live almost a year more than those who never do, according to a study by the Harvard University in America.

Mortality is highest among men who never eat sweets and lowest among men who eat them one to three times a month. The study shows that chocolate in particular has a positive effect. Science attributes this to an ingredient called Phenol that lowers blood pressure, among other things.

In ancient times

In many households you can find stray jars, tins or packs of sugar in the cupboard. All this sweetness is taken for granted nowadays, but it used to be a different story. In the olden days, sweet juices of plants and fruits were used to sweeten food and drink.

Besides plants and fruits, honey is without doubt the oldest sweetener. Honey was used for the preparation of hydromel, a sacred drink that was reserved for a few privileged people. In ancient Greece, honey was an expensive product: half a litre of honey cost as much as a sheep.

Because honey was seen as a sacred substance, it was credited with many healing properties. People thought that consuming honey would lengthen the life span of humans and drive out many illnesses.

Unhealthy?

It is often said that sugar and other sweet things are bad for your health. This is not true, thank goodness, otherwise you would have to forego all those lovely sweet things! Your body needs sugar and everything you eat contributes to your total daily intake of food. Sugar contains carbohydrates that are an important supplier of energy. This does not mean that you can eat sugar all day long; too much is bad for you. Sugar is not usually eaten on its own but in combination with other ingredients and foodstuffs. Jam or sugar in your cup of tea or coffee, for example. These combinations also determine the quality of your food intake every day.

Chocolate

When you hear the word sweet, you not only think of sugar but also of chocolate. Most people love chocolate (especially the female part of the population). This is mostly due to the very pleasant sensation in your mouth when you eat chocolate. This wonderful feeling is entirely created by yourself as the melting point of chocolate is slightly below your body temperature. This is the reason why it melts in your mouth.

In principle, all chocolate is made in the same manner. The major difference is in the type of cocoa bean used, the ratio of the ingredients and a special addition or in other words the tricks of the trade. There is probably no single chocolate maker in the world who will give away his secret ingredient. This is passed on from generation to generation which means that if you do not come from a family of chocolate makers, it will be difficult to unravel this great mystery.

A product can be called chocolate as long as it contains at least 32 per cent cocoa. White chocolate is a different story as it contains no cocoa at all. Officially, it cannot be called chocolate. However, as the structure and taste do resemble that of ordinary chocolate, an exception has been made for white chocolate. One great benefit of the absence of cocoa is that people who are allergic to ordinary chocolate can eat this white confectionery. Thank goodness for that as it would otherwise mean that they would have to miss the delicious taste of chocolate.

Happy

Chocolate makes you feel happy. When you eat chocolate your body produces a chemical called serotonin. This chemical makes you feel happy and relaxed. Unfortunately this feeling is only temporary.

Not very good in bed?
Don't worry, have some chocolate and the problem will be solved. At least, that is what they used to think... French king Louis XV's mistress always gave him a couple of cups of chocolate to drink before they went to bed. Casanova also swore by this drink.

Sweet & Naughty
Coffee snacks

Brownies with walnuts	14
Nougat dark and white	16
Millefeuille pastry with Mascarpone	18
Choux pastry puffs with saffron cream, orange and chocolate sauce	20
Raspberry tea cakes	22
Blueberry muffins with lime curd	24
Apple tartlets with spice	26
Scones with marmalade and cream	28
Muffins with cranberries	30

Brownies with walnuts

For 20 brownies • 200g (7oz) pure chocolate, in pieces • 100g (3.5oz) butter
• 3 eggs • pinch of salt • 75g (2.6oz) sugar • 100g (3.5oz) soft brown sugar
• 2 sachets vanilla sugar • 150g (5.3oz) self-raising flour • 100g (3.5oz) walnuts,
chopped coarsely • butter for greasing • 20 walnuts in halves

1 Preheat the oven to 175° Celsius (350° Fahrenheit, Gas mark 4).
2 Melt the chocolate with the butter in a bain-marie.
3 Whisk the eggs, salt, soft brown sugar and vanilla sugar till it all froths. Then stir in the warm chocolate mixture.
4 Add the self-raising flour and the coarsely chopped walnuts and mix everything well together.
5 Grease a baking tin 30 by 30cm (12 by 12 inches) and scoop the mixture into the tin. Divide it in your mind into pieces 20 and put a walnut on each piece.
6 Bake the brownie for 35 minutes in the preheated oven. Allow it to cool and take it out of the tin. Cut it into 20 pieces.

White and dark nougat

To make white nougat: 220g (7.8oz) sugar • 80g (2.8oz) glucose (available at a patisserie) • 75ml (2.6floz) water • 175g (6.2oz) honey • 2 egg whites, beaten stiff • 250g (8.8oz) white almonds, roasted

1 Cook the sugar with the glucose and the water till it reaches 140°Celsius (275° Fahrenheit). Add the honey and let the mixture cook till the liquid of the honey evaporates. Make sure it does not caramelize.
2 Beat the sugar syrup together with the stiffly beaten egg whites and allow it to cool.
3 Add the roasted almonds to the egg white.
4 Scoop the mixture into a greased tin and allowit to cool.

To make dark nougat: 500g (17.6oz) honey • 50g (1.8oz) glucose (available at a patisserie) • 500g (17.6oz) almonds, roasted

1 Heat the honey with the glucose till it turns brown.
2 Add the roasted almonds to the mixture.
3 Scoop the mixture onto greaseproof paper and allow it to cool.

Mascarpone millefeuille

250g (8.8oz) sugar • 2dl (6.8floz) water • juice of ½ lemon • 2 Granny Smith apples • 2dl (6.8floz) apple juice • 2 sheets of gelatin, soaked in cold water • 2dl (6.8floz) cream, whipped • 200g (7oz) mascarpone • grated peel of ½ lemon • 6 sheets of puff pastry •½ egg white • 150g (5.3oz) icing or soft sugar

1   Preheat the oven to 100°Celsius (212° Fahrenheit, Gas mark just below ¼)
2   Heat 200g (7oz) sugar, water and half the lemon juice in a saucepan till all the sugar has dissolved.
3   Remove the core of 1 apple and slice into very thin pieces. Cover a baking tray with baking paper. Dip the slices of apple in the sugar syrup and dry them for 1½ hours in the preheated oven. Then set the oven to 200 Celsius° (400° Fahrenheit, Gas mark 6).
4   Peel the other apple and cut it into small cubes. Sprinkle these with the remaining lemon juice.
5   Cook and reduce the apple juice to half. Dissolve first the remaining sugar and subsequently the gelatin which should be squeezed out well.
6   Add the cream to the apple juice.
7   Beat the mascarpone loosely. Add the cream mixture, the apple cubes and the grated lemon peel to the mascarpone. Put the mixture in the fridge for 2 hours to stiffen.
8   Cut 24 rounds of 4.5cm (1.75 inches) out of the sheets of puff pastry and prick little holes in them. Bake them for 15 minutes till light brown and ready. Press the raised puff pastry rounds flat with a spatula.
9   Beat the egg whites in a basin till frothy. Sieve the sugar above the egg whites and stir it into a thick, smooth, glistening mixture. Spread the mixture onto the 12 puff pastry rounds.
10 Spread a generous layer of mascarpone cream onto the other 12 puff pastry rounds and press a puff pastry round with the egg white icing on top of it. Serve three millefeuilles per person. If so desired, garnish with the dried apple slices and a little icing or soft sugar.

Please note:
the preparation total preparation time for this recipe is moremore than 2½ hours.

Choux pastry puffs with saffron cream, orange and chocolate sauce

12 choux pastry puffs without filling • 2 oranges in segments • **To make the filling:**
3dl (10.3floz) whipping cream • 50g (1.76oz) sugar • 0.5dl (1.7floz) white wine • pinch of saffron
• 2 sheets of gelatin soaked in water, squeezed out well • **To make the sauce:** 150g (5.3oz) pure chocolate
• 50g (1.76oz) butter • 50g (1.76oz) fine granulated sugar • 1dl (3.5floz) creme fraiche • 3dl (10.2floz) water

1 Make the filling for the choux pastry puffs by whisking the cream together with the sugar till it stiffens.
2 Heat the wine with the saffron on low heat and dissolve the sheets of gelatin in the wine. Let the mixture cool a little and then spoon the gelatin mixture through the cream.
3 Spoon the cream into a piping bag and fill the choux pastry puffs. Put them in the fridge for about half an hour till the cream has stiffened.
4 Melt the chocolate for the sauce in a bain-marie. Melt the butter in the chocolate and dissolve the sugar in this. Take the pan off the heat.
5 Stir the creme fraiche until loose and spoon it through the sauce. Dilute the sauce with water.
6 Serve the choux pastry puffs with the sauce and segments of orange.

Raspberry tea cakes

For 20 cakes: 250g (8.8oz) fresh raspberries • icing or soft sugar • **To make the base:**
70g (2.5oz) butter • 35g (1.25oz) castor sugar • 35g (1.25oz) granulated sugar • 1 egg
• 1g (.04oz) salt • 95g (3.4oz) flour • olive oil for greasing • **To make the filling:**
30g (1.1oz) spice • 10g (0.4oz) butter •1 egg • 4g (0.15oz) water • 4g (0.15oz) patent flour

1   Preheat the oven to 200° Celsius (400°Fahrenheit, Gas mark 6).
2   To make the base, mix the butter and sugar well till it becomes a smooth mixture.
3   Add the egg, stir the mixture till it is smooth again and knead in the salt and flour.
4   Roll out the dough and line small greased cake forms with it.
5   For the filling, mix the spice with the butter. Next, stir in the egg and water and finally the flour.
6   Fill the pastry bases with this mixture and bake them in the preheated oven till the pastry is golden brown.
7   Fill the cakes with raspberries and sprinkle with a little icing sugar.

Blueberry-muffins met lime curd

For 12 muffins · To make the muffins: 200g (7oz) self-raising flour · 1 tsp baking powder
· 1 tbsp lemon peel, grated · 50g (1.76oz) castor sugar · 150g (5.3oz) blueberries (bilberries)
· 75g (2.6oz) butter, melted · 1 egg · 175ml (6floz) milk · olive oil for greasing · **To make the lime curd:**
grated peel and juice of 4 limes · 200g (7oz) castor sugar · 150g (5.3oz) butter · 4 eggs

1 Preheat the oven to 200°Celsius (400° Fahrenheit, Gas mark 6).
2 Mix the self-raising flour together with the baking powder, the grated lemon peel, castor sugar and blueberries.
3 Beat the butter, the egg and the milk together in a different bowl and pour this mixture in one go into the flour mixture.
4 Divide the batter between the 12 greased muffin tins or paper cake cases.
5 Bake the muffins in a preheated oven for 20 minutes till they are nicely browned and ready. Allow to cool and take them out of the tins.
6 To make the curd, bring the lime peel, the lime juice, the sugar and the butter to the boil in a bain-marie. Stir till the sugar is dissolved. Simmer for 3 minutes and stir now and then.
7 Whisk the eggs through the mixture while it is still in the bain-marie. Keep stirring till it begins to thicken. Take the curd off the heat and allow to completely cool. Serve the muffins with the lime curd.

Apple tartlets with spice

2 apples, peeled and cut into small segments • 2 tbsp sugar • juice of one lemon • 1 tbsp butter • 40g (1.4oz) spice • 1 egg yolk • 4 sheets of puff pastry

1   Preheat the oven to 220°Celsius (428°Fahrenheit, Gas mark 7).
2   Sprinkle the apple segments with 1 tablespoon sugar and the lemon juice.
3   Mix butter, spice and egg yolk together well and dip the apple segments in this mixture.
4   Cut a round out of each sheet of puff pastry and prick little holes in them using a fork. Take care not to prick holes in the edges.
5   Divide the apple segments between the puff pastry rounds. Leave 1cm (0.4 inches) of the edge free so they can rise during baking.
6   Sprinkle the tartlets with the remaining sugar and bake them for 16-18 minutes in the preheated oven.

Scones with marmalade and cream

For 12 scones • 100g (3.53oz) castor sugar • 1tsp salt • 275g (9.7oz) self-raising flour
• 60g (2.1oz) ice-cold butter • 2 eggs • 1 egg yolk • 125ml (4.3floz) milk • flour • butter for greasing
• **To make the orange marmalade** • 1kg (35.3oz) oranges, well-cleaned • 1dl (3.4floz) water
• 500g (17.6oz) preserving sugar • **To make the clotted cream:** 125g (4.4oz) mascarpone
• 1 tsp sugar •125ml (4.3floz) cream, beaten to soft peaks

1 Preheat the oven to 220°Celsius (428°Fahrenheit, Gas mark 7).
2 Mix the sugar and salt together with the flour. Mix the butter with the flour by using two knives to cut it into small pieces till you have a crumbly mixture.
3 Whisk 1 egg together with the egg yolk and the milk and add it to the dough. Make sure your hands are cool before you knead it into supple but sticky dough.
4 On a working space, dusted with flour, roll out the dough till it is approx. 2cm (0.79 inches) thick and then cut out rounds. Put these on a greased baking tin.
5 Beat the remaining egg and coat the scones with this. Bake them for about 20 minutes in the preheated oven till they are light brown and well-baked.
6 For the orange marmalade, use a parer to peel the rind (without the pith) of two oranges and cut this into thin strips. Squeeze two oranges (keep the juice for later) and then cook the strips for about 5 minutes in the water. Allow to drain.
7 Peel 1 orange thickly, cut the flesh of the fruit away from the pith and cut into small pieces. Cut the rest of the fruit into slices and collect the juice.
8 Put everything together with the preserving sugar in a large pan and bring to the boil. Let it cook well for about 4 minutes, stir regularly.
9 Spoon the marmalade into a clean jar and close this immediately. Place the jar upside down and let it cool.
10 To make the clotted cream, add the mascarpone and sugar to the cream and whisk till it is thick. Serve the scones with marmalade and cream.

Muffins with cranberries

For 12 muffins • butter for greasing • 250g (8.8oz) flour • 200g (7oz) sugar • 2 tsp baking powder
• ½ tsp salt • 3 eggs (medium-sized) • 1dl (3.5floz) creme fraiche • 50g (1.76oz) butter, melted • 1 tsp lemon
peel, grated • 1tbsp lemon juice • 150g (5.3oz) cranberries • **To make the upper layer:** 1 tsp cinnamon
• 2 tbsp flour • 50g (1.76oz) butter • 50g (1.76oz) brown sugar

1 Preheat the oven to 200° Celsius (400° Fahrenheit, Gas mark 6). Grease 12 muffin forms with butter.
2 Sieve the flour, the sugar, the baking powder and the salt above a mixing bowl and then mix all the ingredients together well.
3 Whisk the eggs. Stir the creme fraiche till it becomes fluid and add this with the melted butter, the lemon peel and the lemon juice to the whisked eggs.
4 Fold the egg mixture into the flour till is just slightly mixed. Spoon the cranberries through the mixture and divide the batter between the muffin tins.
5 Mix the ingredients for the upper layer in a food processor until they have a granular texture. Give each of the muffins an equal amount.
6 Bake the muffins for about 20 minutes in the preheated oven till they are done. Use a pricker to see if they are ready, it should come out of the muffin without any traces of batter.
7 Let the muffins cool before serving.

Slow & Sweet
Brunch

French toast with pears and almonds	34
Sweet nut bread with dates	36
Corn cakes with mango chutney	38
Sweet rolls	40
Crêpes with honey	42
Panettone	44
Chocolate French toast with pistachio nuts	46

French toast with pears and almonds

For 8 portions: 2 eggs • 2.5dl (8.5floz) milk • 8 slices white bread, without crust • 30g (1.1oz) butter • 1 tbsp sugar • For garnishing: 4 tbsp liquid honey • 45g (1.6oz) shredded almonds

1   In a large bowl, beat the eggs through the milk with a whisk.
2   Pour the contents of the bowl into a deep plate and coat the slices of bread with the egg mixture.
3   Heat a little butter in a frying pan at medium heat. Fry the slices of bread for 3 minutes on both sides. While frying, sprinkle them with a little sugar. Take the French toast out of the pan and sprinkle them with honey and dust with almonds.

TIP French toast is also delicious with only a dusting of cinnamon. Or vary with apple(s); take out the core and slice the apples. Fry the slices for 5 minutes with a knob of butter in the frying pan on a medium heat. Turn them over regularly and sprinkle cinnamon on top half way through frying. Put the apple slices on top of the French toast.

Sweet nut bread with dates

150g (5.3oz) finely chopped mixed nuts (walnuts, pistachio nuts, hazel nuts, almonds etc.)
• 50g (1.76oz) dates, cut into pieces • 50g (1.76oz) butter, melted • 100g (3.53oz) self-raising flour
• 80g (2.8oz) cane sugar • 3 eggs • salt

1. Mix the chopped nuts, the pieces of date, the melted butter, the flour, the cane sugar and the eggs with a pinch of salt together to make a smooth batter.
2. Spoon the batter into a greased square glass dish.
3. Cover the nut bread and place it for 8 minutes in a microwave oven set to full power.
4. Let the nut bread rest for 5 minutes and the take it out of the dish. Cut the bread into triangles or into another shape.

Corn cakes with mango chutney

100g (3.53oz) flour • 1 egg • 50ml (1.7floz) milk • salt and pepper • 1 tin of maize (corn)
• olive oil, extra pure • **To make the mango chutney:** 1 mango, peeled and cut into pieces
• 1 orange, flesh cut into pieces and the rind in slivers • 1cm (0.4 inches) fresh ginger, grated
• 1 tbsp lemon vinegar • 1 tbsp sugar • 2 cloves

1 Mix the flour and the egg together in a bowl. Then add, while mixing, the milk drop by drop. Flavour the batter with salt and pepper and mix in the kernels of corn (maize). Let the batter rest for a while.
2 To make the chutney, bring all the ingredients slowly to the boil in a pan. Simmer for about 30 minutes. Stir regularly to avoid burning.
3 Heat the olive oil in a non-stick pan. Make 6 small cakes out of the corn (maize) batter. Fry them for about 3 minutes till golden brown. Serve the corn cakes with mango chutney.

Sweet Rolls

2 ½ tsp dry yeast • 1 tsp sugar • 125ml (4.3floz) lukewarm water • 2.5dl (8.5floz) full cream milk • 1 large egg, whisked • 4 tbsp butter, melted • 1 tsp aniseed • 1 tsp salt • 60g (2.2oz) granulated sugar • 750g (26.5oz) flour, sieved • greaseproof paper • brown sugar, sieved • 2 tbsp cinnamon

1 Mix the yeast, sugar and water together.
2 Next mix the milk and the egg and 2 tablespoons melted butter together. Stir in the aniseed, salt and granulated sugar. Add the yeast mixture and mix everything together well.
3 Fold in the flour gradually to make soft dough. Cover and let the dough rest in a warm, draught-free place till the volume has doubled.
4 Put the dough on a work space dusted with flour and divide into 24 equal pieces. Mould into little balls and put them on grease proof paper on a baking tray. Cover loosely and let the balls rest for one more hour in a warm draught-free place so they double in size.
5 Preheat the oven to 200° Celsius (400°Fahrenheit, Gas mark 6).
6 Coat the rolls with the rest of the melted butter and dust them with sugar and cinnamon. Bake them in the preheated oven for 15 minutes.

Please note:
the total preparation time for this
recipe is more than 2 hours.

Crêpes with honey

For 4-6 people • 250g (8.8oz) flour • 3dl (10.3floz) milk • 2 eggs • ½ tsp salt • sugar • olive oil • 2 apples, cut into slices • honey • castor sugar

1 Sieve the flour above a bowl. Add the milk gradually. Keep on stirring to prevent lumps forming.
2 Add the eggs and stir these into the batter. The batter should pour off the spoon. Next stir salt and 1 teaspoon sugar through the batter.
3 Heat a generous amount of oil in a non-stick frying pan till the oil starts to smoke slightly. Pour a little batter into the frying pan and tilt it so the oil is evenly distributed.
4 Fry the crêpes first on one side then on the other till they are golden brown. Put the crêpes on a dish and keep them warm while you fry the rest.
5 Fry the slices of apple lightly on both sides. In the meantime, shake a thin layer of 'ordinary' sugar over them.
6 Portion the crêpes onto the plates. Sprinkle a little honey over them and dust with a little castor sugar.
7 Garnish the crêpes with the sugared slices of apple. Serve hot.

Panettone

25g (0.88oz) dry yeast • 1.5dl (5.7floz) milk • 500g (17.6oz) flour • 1 egg • 2 egg yolks • 80g (2.8oz) (vanilla) sugar • 1 1/2 tbsp salt • 120g (4.2oz) (approximately) melted butter for greasing • 150g (5.3oz) raisins • peel of 1 lemon, grated • peel of 1 orange, grated • 10g (0.35oz) butter

1   Mix the yeast with 2 tablespoons milk and 1 tablespoon flour till it becomes a smooth mixture.
2   Whisk the egg together with the 2 egg yolks and stir in the sugar and the salt. Mix the melted butter with the yeast mixture and stir in the egg mixture.
3   Mix the yeast mixture together with the rest of the flour and add the remaining milk. Knead this into a smooth dough. Cover the dough with a piece of greased foil and let it rise in a warm place for 2 hours.
4   Knead the dough once more. Mix in the raisins, lemon and orange peel and let it rise for another 2 hours.
5   Preheat the oven to 180° Celsius (350°Fahrenheit, Gas mark 4).
6   Cover the outside of a cake tin with aluminium foil till you have a sturdy collar that is 15cm (6 inches) high in total.
7   Knead the dough into a ball and put that in the form. Let the dough rise for half an hour.
8   Put the butter carefully on the dough and bake the panettone for 1 hour in the preheated oven till ready (prick in the panettone with a pricker, if it is ready it will come out clean).

TIP when organizing a dinner party, it is a good idea to make the dough a day beforehand.

Please note:
the total preparation time for this
recipe is more than 6 hours.

Chocolate French toast
with pistachio nuts

For 8 portions · **To make the French toast:** 2 eggs · 2.5dl (8.5floz) milk
· 8 slices white bread · I tbsp olive oil · I tbsp sugar · **For garnishing:** 2 dl (6.8floz) chocolate sauce
· 150g (5.3oz) pistachio nuts, chopped · icing sugar (soft sugar)

1   Using a whisk beat the eggs through the milk in a large bowl.
2   Pour the contents into a deep plate and coat the slices of bread with the egg mixture.
3   Heat the olive oil in a frying pan at medium heat. Fry the slices of bread for 3 minutes on each side and sprinkle a little
    sugar over them during frying. Take them out of the frying pan.
4   Spoon the chocolate sauce over the French toast and sprinkle the pistachio nuts on top.
5   Garnish the French toast with a little icing sugar.

Sweety-pie
Cakes & Pies

Almond-peach tartlets

For 8 pieces • butter or oil for greasing • 8 sheets of puff pastry • 4 ripe peaches, peeled and stoned • 50g (1.76oz) pure chocolate • **To make the filling:** 4 eggs, divided • grated peel of ½ lemon • 40ml (1.4floz) coffee liqueur • 250g (8.8oz) finely chopped almonds • a little lemon juice

1   Preheat the oven to 200° Celsius (400° Fahrenheit, Gas mark 6).
2   To make the filling, whisk the eggs with the lemon peel and the sugar. Mix in the coffee liqueur and the finely chopped almonds.
3   Whisk the egg whites stiff with a few drops of lemon juice and spoon this through the almond mixture.
4   Grease 8 little round baking tins with butter and line them with puff pastry. Divide the filling over the tins and place a peach in the middle with the round side up. Bake the tartlets for 5 minutes in a preheated oven.
5   Let the tartlets cool. Melt the chocolate in a bain-marie.
6   Make a piping bag out of baking paper and pipe a stripy pattern over the tartlets.

Yogurt flan with bilberries

To make the dough • 60g (2.2oz) almonds, chopped • 100g (3.53oz) butter • 3 tbsp brown sugar
• 1 egg • 150g (5.3oz) flour • oil for greasing • **To make the filling:** 100g (3.53oz) sugar
• juice and grated peel of 1 orange • 5 sheets gelatin, soaked in water • 200g (7oz) bilberries (blueberries)
• 2l (68floz) yogurt, hung in a a tea towel for a few hours to drain (to make curds)

1 Preheat the oven to 190° Celsius (375°Fahrenheit, Gas mark 5).
2 To make the dough, mix the almonds, the butter and the sugar in a blender for a short while.
3 Add the egg and the flour. Use the pulse button and let the machine rotate shortly a few times till the mixture becomes
   crumbly. Knead and mix it with the hand till it becomes a dough.
4 Line a greased cake tin with a layer of dough that is about 2cm (0.8i nches) thick.
5 Put the cake tin with the dough in the fridge for 20 minutes and then bake it in the oven for about 20 minutes.
6 To make the filling, cook the orange juice with the sugar till the sugar has dissolved.
7 Add the gelatin and wait till it dissolves.
8 Stir this mixture through the curds together with the bilberries and then fill the flan with it.

Please note:
the total preparation time for
this recipe is more than 7 hours.

Cheesecake with orange and almonds

160g (5.6oz) soft butter • 120g (4.2oz) sugar • 6 eggs, divided • 500g (17.6oz) mascarpone
• 400g (14oz) cottage (or cream) cheese • grated peel of 4 oranges • 200g (7oz) almonds, grounded
• 150g (5.3oz) flour, sieved • 300g (10.6oz) white chocolate, either grated or in small pieces
• 1 cake tin 26cm (10.25 inches) diameter, greased • icing (or soft sugar)

1   Preheat the oven to 180° Celsius (350°Fahrenheit, Gas mark 4).
2   Beat the butter with the sugar till it is pale.
3   Whisk the egg yolks and spoon these together with the mascarpone, cottage cheese, orange peel, almonds and the flour through the butter mixture.
4   Whisk the egg whites till they are really stiff and spoon them together with the chocolate through the mixture.
5   Spoon the mixture into the cake tin and put it in the middle of the oven.
6   Bake the cake for 50 minutes till done. Prick it in the middle with a satay stick; if it comes out dry, the cake is ready.
7   Turn off the oven but leave the cake in there for another 5 minutes with the door open. Sprinkle with icing sugar.
8   Let the cake cool a little and then cut into slices. Eat it when it is still just warm.

Please note:
the total preparation time for
this recipe is more than 1 hour.

Apple crumble tartlets

For 6 tartlets • For the crumble: 180g (6.35 oz) flour • 225g (7.94 oz) sugar
• 100g (3.53 oz) butter, cold and cubed • Butter or oil for greasing • **For the filling:**
6 large cooking apples sliced into 2cm (0.79 inches) pieces • 100g (3.35 oz) sugar • 2 tbsp lemon juice
• 1 tsp cinnamon powder • 2 tbsp walnuts, chopped

1   Preheat the oven to 180°C (350°F, gas mark 4).
2   Combine the flour and sugar and add the cold, diced butter.
3   Make the crumble by rubbing ingredients together with your fingertips.
4   Combine the apple pieces, sugar, lemon juice, cinnamon and walnuts.
5   Portion the apple over the bottom of 6 greased tartlet tins.
6   Arrange the crumble over the top of each and cook the tartlets for about 40 minutes in the preheated oven.

Lemon cake

To make the base: 50g (1.76oz) butter • I tbsp lemon marmalade (or lemon jam)
• I pack spicy biscuits (without ginger), ground in the food processor • **To make the filling:**
juice of 3 lemons • 10 sheets gelatin, soaked in cold water • 400g (14oz) cream cheese
• 5dl (17floz) whole yogurt • 100g (3.53oz) soft sugar • I sachet vanilla sugar
• **To make the lemon slices:** 300g (10.6oz) sugar • I lemon, in thin slices

1   To make the base, melt the butter and mix this together with the lemon marmalade and the ground biscuits.
2   Line a cake tin with plastic film and cover the base with the biscuit mixture. Press it down well.
3   Make the lemon slices, bring water with the sugar to the boil on high heat. Cook till the mixture is clear.
4   Turn the heat down and put the slices of lemon in the syrup for 30 minutes. The mixture should not boil.
5   Take the slices out of the syrup with a skimmer and allow to cool.
6   To make the filling, heat the lemon juice and dissolve the squeezed out gelatin in it.
7   Mix the cheese, yogurt, soft sugar and vanilla sugar and stir in the lemon juice with gelatin.
8   Pour the filling into the cake tin. Smooth the top of the cake and put it in the fridge for 4 hours to stiffen.
9   Cover the top of the cake with the lemon slices.

Please note:
the total preparation time for
this recipe is more than 4 hours.

Apple dumpling with cinnamon

80g (2.1oz) butter • 80g (2.1oz) flour • 80g (2.1oz) soft brown sugar • 2dl (6.9floz) milk
• 2 eggs • salt • firm, sour apples, peeled, core removed with a apple corer
• 4 tbsp sugar • 4 tsp cinnamon

1 Preheat the oven to 225°Celsius (437°Fahrenheit, Gas mark 7).
2 Melt the butter in a pan and stir in the flour, sugar, eggs and a pinch of salt. Keep stirring till you have a smooth batter.
3 Spoon 1 tablespoon sugar and 1 teaspoon of cinnamon into each apple.
4 Put the apples in a baking tin and pour in the batter.
5 Place the baking tin in the preheated oven for about 50 minutes.

Please note:
the total preparation time for
this recipe is more than 1 hour.

Vanilla crumble flan

For the dough: 2 tbsp soft butter • 2 tbsp sugar • 150g (5.29oz) flour
• 1dl (3.4floz) lukewarm milk • ½ sachet dried yeast • **To make the filling:** 80g (2.82oz) sugar
• 1 vanilla pod • 5dl (17floz) milk • 3 eggs, the egg yolks • 1 tbsp cornflour (cornstarch)
• **For the crumble:** 75g (2.65oz) butter • 150g (5.29oz) flour • 100g (3.53oz) soft brown sugar

1   Mix all the ingredients for the dough well and knead them into supple dough. Cover it and let it rise till the volume has doubled. Knead it again and let it rise for another 20 minutes.
2   Roll out a round piece of about 28cm (11 inches) in diameter. Line a baking tin with a diameter of 26cm (10.25 inches) with the dough.
2   For the filling, mix half the amount of sugar with the vanilla pod and 3dl (10.3floz) milk. Bring this to the boil, take the pan off the heat, cover the milk and let it infuse for 20 minutes.
3   Preheat the oven to 180° Celsius (350°Fahrenheit, Gas mark 4).
5   Scrape the vanilla pod clean and put the marrow back in the pan.
6   Whisk the egg yolk with the remaining sugar till it is stiff.
7   Beat a little milk through the egg yolk and add this to the vanilla milk.
8   Mix 1dl (3.5floz) milk with the cornflour and add this to the vanilla milk too.
9   Bring the vanilla milk to the boil and whisk it together when it has been taken off the heat.
10 To make the crumble, rub the butter, flour and sugar together with the fingers till it becomes crumbly.
11 Fill the flan base with the filling and cover it with the crumble.
12 Bake the cake for 18 minutes in the oven till ready.

Please note:
the total preparation time for
this recipe is more than 1 hour.

Strawberry cakes with mascarpone

2 eggs • 110g (3.9oz) sugar • marrow of 1 vanilla pod • 75g (2.6oz) flour, sieved
• 1 tsp baking powder • 1 tbsp butter • 75ml (2.6floz) milk • butter for greasing
• **To make the filling:** 2.5dl (8.8floz) whipping cream • 2 tbsp sugar • 250g (8.8oz) mascarpone
• 2 tbsp strawberry liqueur • 250g (8.8oz) strawberries (large ones halved) • icing sugar (or soft sugar)

1   Preheat the oven to 180° Celsius (350°Fahrenheit, Gas mark 4).
2   Mix the eggs, sugar and the vanilla pod marrow with the blender until the mixture becomes thick and frothy.
3   Heat the butter with the milk. Let it cool a little before mixing it with the egg mixture.
4   Grease a cake tin with butter and line the tin with baking paper. Spoon the batter into the tin. Bake the cake for about 30 minutes (prick in the cake with a pricker, the cake is ready when it comes out clean). Let the cake cool for 5 minutes in the cake tin.
5   Take the cake out of the tin and cut out 12 rounds.
6   Whisk the cream into soft peaks for the filling. Stir in the mascarpone and the liqueur.
7   Spread the filling onto the 12 rounds. Make two-tier cakes by putting one round on top of the other. Garnish with the remaining strawberries and dust with icing sugar.

Bilberry pie

600g (21oz) bilberries (blueberries) • 125g (4.4oz) self-raising powder • 25ml (0.85floz) olive oil • 50ml (1.7floz) milk • 25ml (0.85flz) water • 150g (5.29oz) sugar • 25g (0.88oz) flour • 1 tsp grated lemon rind • Pie dish or other baking form

1   Preheat the oven to 180° Celsius (350°Fahrenheit, Gas mark 4).
2   Mix the self-raising flour with the olive oil, the milk and the water. Knead the mixture into a supple dough.
3   Divide the dough into 2 pieces and roll these into circles of about 26 cm (10.25 inches) diameter between greaseproof paper.
4   Mix the bilberries (blueberries) with the sugar, flour and lemon rind.
5   Put 1 dough circle in a greased pie dish and cover the dough with bilberries(blueberries).
6   Lay the other dough circle on top. Carve a cross in the middle and cover the dough with aluminium foil.
7   Bake the pie for about 20 minutes in the oven. Remove the foil and bake for about 12 minutes till the crust is nice and brown.

Please note:
the total preparation time for
this recipe is more than 5 hour.

Fruit pie

To make the dough: 175g (6.2oz) flour • 80g (2.8oz) butter, at room temperature
• ice cold water • **For the filling:** I egg yolk, beaten • 2 heaped tbsp cornflour (cornstarch)
• 750g (26.5oz) cleaned fruit (gooseberries, peaches, apricots, strawberries, plums or cherries)
• 75g (2.65oz) sugar • **For garnishing:** I egg white, whisked • 50g (1.76) granulated sugar

1 Sieve the flour above a large bowl and rub the butter in with your fingertips till it looks like coarse bread crumbs. Sprinkle enough water onto it to make a dough that sticks together. Knead the dough lightly, wrap tightly in plastic film and put in the fridge for 30 minutes.
2 Preheat the oven to 200° Celsius (400°Fahrenheit, Gas mark 6).
3 Roll out the dough on a work space dusted with flour. Make a dough circle which is about 35cm (13.8inches) in diameter. Turn the dough during rolling a quarter turn every now and then. The edges should look a little ragged. Fold the dough over the rolling pin and place it on a greased baking tray.
4 Coat the middle of the dough circle with egg yolk and sprinkle cornflour over it. Fold the dough edges over the fruit, if it breaks just press the dough together again. It should look a little untidy.
6 Brush the top of the dough with the egg white and sprinkle sugar over it.
7 Bake the pie in a preheated oven for about 35 minutes till it is golden brown.

Please note:
the total preparation time for
this recipe is more than I hour.

Orange cake

For one cake (8 people) • **To make the cake:** 100g (3.53oz) butter, cut into small pieces
• 250g (8.8oz) flour • 2 egg yolks • 50g (1.76oz) sugar • pinch of salt • butter or oil for greasing
• **To make the filling:** 60g (2.1oz) butter, melted • 5 eggs, whisked • juice of 5 oranges
• 200g (7oz) sugar • **To make the garnishing:** 2 oranges, washed and cut into very thin slices
• 75g (2.65oz) sugar • 2.5dl (8.5floz) water • **To make the syrup:** 2 tbsp orange juice • 60g (2.1oz) sugar

1   Preheat the oven to180° Celsius (350°Fahrenheit, Gas mark 4).
2   To make the cake, mix the butter and flour well together.
3   Add the egg yolks, the sugar and the salt and mix everything into a light kneadable cake dough.
4   Grease a cake tin, measuring 26-28cm (10.25-11inches) in diameter, with butter. Place the cake dough in it and set apart.
5   To make the filling, mix the melted butter, the eggs, the orange juice and the sugar well. Heat the mixture in a bain-marie and keep stirring till it becomes thick. This can take some time (5 to 10 minutes). Do not try to speed up the process by turning up the heat.
6   Pour the filling on top of the cake dough in the tin. Put the cake tin in the preheated oven. At the end of the baking time, use a pricker to prick the base to see if it is done. If the pricker comes out clean, the base is ready. Take the cake tin out of the oven and let it cool.
7   To make the garnishing, bring the slices of orange with the sugar and the water to the boil in a pan. Let it cook till the orange slices are done. Make sure they are not overcooked as they will then not be easy to work with.
8   Heat the orange juice with the sugar to make the syrup.
9   Lay the orange slices on top of the cake so it is completely covered. Pour the warm syrup over it. Let it cool before serving.

Mandarin slice

9 mandarins • juice of 1 lime • 10 sheets of gelatin, soaked in cold water • 4 eggs, divided
• 175g (6.2oz) sugar • 4.5dl (15.5floz) yogurt • 2dl (6.8floz) cottage cream • 3 tbsp Cointreau

1   Grate the rind of 2 mandarins and squeeze them with another 4 mandarins.
2   Peel 2 mandarins; cut away the pith and slice into small pieces. Keep one mandarin for garnishing.
3   Mix the mandarin and the lime juice and heat this up. Squeeze out the gelatin sheets and dissolve them in the warm juice.
4   Whisk the egg yolks with the sugar till they are white and foamy. Whisk the egg whites till they are very stiff.
5   Mix the yogurt with cottage cream and the cooled juice. Spoon the whisked egg yolks, the grated mandarin peel, the pieces of mandarin and the Cointreau through this mixture. Finally, carefully mix in the egg whites.
6   Line a cake tin with plastic film and spoon the yogurt mix into it. Make the surface smooth. Leave in the fridge for at least 5 hours to stiffen.
7   Garnish the cake with segments of mandarin, optionally dipped in melted chocolate, and cut the cake into wedges.

 Please note:
the total preparation time to make
this recipe is more than 5 hours.

Apple tartlets with spicy biscuits and buttermilk sorbet

To make the tartlets: 100g (3.53oz) spicy biscuits • 2 tbsp butter • 1 tbsp brown sugar • 3 apples, peeled and cut into segments • 80g (2.8oz) almond paste
• **To make the buttermilk sorbet:** 2dl (6.8floz) champagne • 2 tbsp honey • 80g (2.8oz) sugar • 1dl (3.4floz) lemon juice • 5dl (17.3floz) buttermilk

1   Preheat the oven to 200° Celsius (400°Fahrenheit, Gas mark 6).
2   To make the tartlets, crumble the spicy biscuits and mix them together with 1 tablespoon butter and the brown sugar.
3   Divide the mixture between 4 little cake moulds.
4   Mix the apple segments together with the almond paste and 1 tablespoon butter and fill the cake moulds with this.
5   Bake the tartlets for 30 minutes in the preheated oven till done.
6   To make the buttermilk sorbet, bring the champagne, honey and sugar to the boil and then allow to cool.
7   Add the lemon juice to the buttermilk and spin in an ice machine. Serve the sorbet with the apple tartlets.

TIP also delicious with cinnamon ice-cream.

Meringue with caramel sauce

To make the meringue: 4 egg whites • 1 pinch of salt • 4 tbsp cold water
• 250g (8.8oz) sugar • 1 sachet vanilla sugar • 1 tbsp white wine vinegar • 4 tbsp maize (corn) flour
• 1 tbsp oil • **To make the filling:** 100g (3.53oz) hazelnuts, roasted and chopped
• 1-2 tbsp nut liqueur • 4dl (13.75floz) cream, whisked into soft peaks • 400g (14.1oz) summer fruit
• 1 lemon, the juice • **To make the caramel sauce:** 250g (8.8oz) sugar • 250g (8.8oz) cream

1   Preheat the oven to 150°Celsius (300° Fahrenheit, Gas mark 2).
2   To make the meringue, whisk the egg whites with the salt till stiff. Add, while whisking, the water drop by drop and then the sugar. Mix in the vanilla sugar, the vinegar and the maize flour.
4   Grease two equal sized tins with a little oil. Divide the meringue over the tins. Make a smooth layer in one and a 'heaped' one in the other. Bake the meringue for about 35 minutes in a preheated oven.
5   Mix all the ingredients for the filling well.
6   Place the baked meringues on top of each other, the 'heaped' one at the top and the filling in-between.
7   To make the filling, let the sugar caramelize for 5 minutes in a pan. Do not stir.
8   Deglaze the sauce by adding the cream and cook on low heat till everything has dissolved.
9   Cover the meringue with the sauce just before serving.

Sweet Surrender
Chocolate

Chocolate creams

For 25-30 chocolate creams • 300-500g (10.5-17.6oz) chocolate, at the correct blending temperature • **To make the filling:** 80g (2.8oz) sugar • 7 tbsp water • 1 egg • 100g (3.53oz) butter, at room temperature • 2g (.07oz) instant coffee • 85g (3oz) milk chocolate, melted • 35g (1.25oz) hazelnut paste

1   To make the filling, bring the sugar with 5 tablespoons water to the boil in a pan. Let it boil for 1 minute.
2   Whisk the egg smooth and then dribble in the hot sugar syrup.
3   Beat the butter slowly, little by little, through this mixture. Whisk till it is smooth.
4   Dissolve the instant coffee in 2 tablespoons water and add this to the creme.
5   Mix the melted milk chocolate with the hazelnut paste.
6   Put the blended chocolate with the help of a brush into the chocolate creme forms. Repeat this twice so the edge is thick enough.
7   Fill a piping bag with the coffee creme and pipe a layer of 4mm (0.15inches) in the chocolate creams.
8   Pipe the chocolate creme up to 2mm under the edge. Let it stiffen for 5-10 minutes in the fridge.
9   Close the chocolate creams with the blended chocolate. Let them cool for 30 minutes in the fridge. Take them out of the forms with a few taps.

TIP You can also buy ready-made chocolate cups. And how about trying a white chocolate filling?
Combine 50ml (1.69 floz) cream and 1 egg yolk. Add 100g (3.35oz) melted white chocolate and whisk briskly for about 1 minute. Add 1 tablespoon of Cointreau.

Please note:
the total preparation time to make
this recipe is more than 1 hour.

Chocolate mousse

150g (5.3oz) pure chocolate • 5 egg yolks • 6 tsp sugar • 2.5dl (8.7floz) cream
• 6 egg whites • 1 tbsp Tia Maria or another coffee liqueur

1   Melt the chocolate in a bain-marie.
2   Whisk the egg yolks till you have a stiff, frothy mixture. Add this to the melted chocolate.
3   Whisk the cream till it almost stiff.
4   Beat the egg whites till they form stiff peaks.
5   Add the Tia Maria to the chocolate. Then spoon the cream and the egg whites through the chocolate.
6   Pour the mousse into 4 small bowls and put these in the fridge 1 hour before serving.

Please note:
the total preparation time to make
this recipe is more than 1 hour.

Simple chocolate cake

For 6-8 people • 200g (7oz) pure chocolate • 200g (7oz) butter • 250g (8.8oz) sugar • 5 eggs • 1 tbsp flour • 2 tbsp orange peel, grated

1 Preheat the oven to 190° Celsius (375° Fahrenheit, Gas mark 5).
2 Melt the chocolate with the butter in the microwave or in a bain-marie.
3 Add the sugar. Take the mixture off the heat and let it cool.
4 Sir in the eggs, one by one.
5 Add the flour and the orange peel and stir till you have a smooth mixture.
6 Put the mixture in a cake tin of 20cm (8inches) diameter and bake it for about 25 minutes in the preheated oven. The cake should still be slightly soft in the middle.
7 Take the cake out of the form and let it cool.

Chocolate cake with mascarpone

To make the chocolate cake: 4 eggs • 100g (3.53oz) icing sugar (or soft sugar) • 30g (1oz) cocoa (plus extra for garnishing) • To make the mascarpone mixture: 3 egg yolks • 500g (17.6oz) mascarpone • 75g (2.6oz) sugar • 1dl (3.5floz) Grand Marnier (plus extra for sprinkling) • 2 tbsp white chocolate

1 Preheat the oven to180° Celsius (350°Fahrenheit, Gas mark 4).
2 To make the cake, whisk the eggs with sugar till they are pale in colour.
3 Melt the butter and let this cool a little. Stir in the flour and cocoa.
4 Spoon the flour mixture through the eggs.
5 Line a baking tray with greaseproof paper and spread the chocolate mixture on top.
6 Bake the chocolate mixture for about 10 minutes in the preheated oven till the cake is ready and let it cool. Cut it into pieces.
7 To make the mascarpone mixture, mix the egg yolks with the mascarpone and whisk everything well together. Then mix in the sugar and the Grand Marnier.
8 Melt the white chocolate and mix this through the mascarpone mixture.
9 Take 4 glasses and put a slice of cake at the bottom of each glass. Sprinkle the cake with Grand Marnier.
10 Spoon the mascarpone onto the cake and dust with cocoa powder.

Chocolate layer cake

For 6-8 people • **To make the cake dough:** 150g (5.3oz) chocolate
• 130g (4.6oz) butter • 180g (6.3oz) icing sugar (or soft sugar) • 6 eggs, divided • 130g (4.6oz) flour
• 1 tsp baking powder • **To make the filling:** 2dl (7floz) cream • 400g (14oz) white chocolate
• **To make the glazing:** 200g (7oz) pure chocolate • 125g (4.4oz) butter • 1 tbsp syrup

1 Heat the oven to 180° Celsius (350°Fahrenheit, Gas mark 4).
2 To make the cake dough, melt the chocolate in a bain-marie and let it cool till it is just fluid.
3 Mix the butter with half of the icing sugar till it becomes creamy. Add the egg yolks one by one. Pour in the chocolate and mix everything well.
4 Sieve the flour together with the baking powder above the chocolate mixture and fold it into the flour.
5 Whisk the egg whites with the rest of the sugar into stiff peaks and fold this in three parts through the chocolate mixture. Transfer the batter into the cake tin. Bake the cake for about 1 hour in a preheated oven till a pricker comes out of the cake dry. Let the cake cool.
6 To make the filling, heat the cream and pour this over the white chocolate. Melt the chocolate while you keep stirring well and then let the mixture cool.
7 Cut the cake across twice so there are three slices. Spread the white chocolate mixture on two slices. Put the slices on top of the other. Place the slice without chocolate mixture on top. Put the cake in a cool place so the filling stiffens.
8 To make the glazing, melt chocolate, butter and syrup in a bain-marie.
9 Spread a little glazing on the cake and put it the freezer for 10 minutes so the chocolate hardens.
10 Finally, spread a thick layer of chocolate glazing on the cake (put the cake on a rack with a bowl underneath to catch any excess chocolate). Let the glazing harden in a cool place.

Please note:
the total preparation time for
this recipe is more than 1 hour.

White chocolate truffle cake

For 8-12 slices of cake • **To make the base:** 2 eggs • 50g (1.76oz) fine granulated sugar
• 50g (1.76oz) flour, sieved • 50g (1.76oz) white chocolate • **To make the upper layer:**
3dl (10.5floz) cream • 350g (12.3oz) white chocolate, in pieces • 250g (8.8oz) cream cheese (Mon Chou)
• **To make the chocolate shavings:** 100g (3.53oz) pure chocolate • 1tbsp cocoa

1 Preheat the oven to 180° Celsius (350°Fahrenheit, Gas mark 4).
2 To make the base, mix the eggs and the sugar till you have an airy, light yellow mixture. Fold in the flour.
3 Melt the chocolate in a bain-marie and mix it through the cake dough.
4 Pour the batter into a greased cake tinof about 20cm (8 inches) in diameter. Bake the base for about 25 minutes in
   the preheated oven till it is ready. Let the base cool.
5 To make the upper layer, bring the cream to the boil. Stir well to stop the cream burning on the bottom of the pan.
   Let the cream cool a little and then add the white chocolate, piece by piece. Keep stirring till all the chocolate has
   dissolved. Stir the cheese till creamy and add this to the chocolate mixture.
6 Pour the mixture onto the cake base and put the cake in the fridge for two hours to stiffen.
7 To make the chocolate shavings, melt the pure chocolate in a bain-marie. Pour the chocolate onto a marble (or synthetic)
   slab and spread it into a thin layer with a spatula. Let the chocolate cool and harden (not in the fridge). Make shavings
   by putting a knife under the chocolate at a 25 degree angle. Place these in the middle of the cake. Dust with cocoa using
   a tea strainer.

Please note:
the total preparation time for
this recipe is more than 3 hour.

Chocolate cake with cumquat

125g (4.5oz) pure chocolate, in pieces • 125g (4.5oz) butter, cut into cubes • 2 eggs, separated • 50g (1.76oz) sugar • butter for greasing • extra flour • icing sugar (or soft sugar) • **To make the compote:** 1.5dl (5.2floz) water • 3dl (10.4floz) orange juice • 250g (8.8oz) sugar • 350g (12.3oz) cumquats, cut into small pieces

1   To make the compote, heat the water with the orange juice and the sugar.
2   Add the pieces of cumquat and let the mixture simmer for 1 hour. After an hour, let the compote cool.
3   Preheat the oven to 220° Celsius (425° Fahrenheit, Gas mark 7).
4   Melt the chocolate with the butter in a bain-marie, do not stir too much.
5   Whisk the egg yolks with the sugar till they are white and creamy.
6   Whisk the egg whites till they are stiff.
7   Add the whisked egg yolks, the flour and the egg white to the chocolate and fold everything carefully together. Turn the bowl while doing so.
8   Grease 4 soufflé tins with butter and dust them with flour. Spoon the chocolate mixture into them. Bake the cakes in the preheated oven for 10 minutes.
9   Sprinkle the cakes with a little icing sugar and serve with the cumquat compote.

TIP: other fruit such as oranges can also be used instead of cumquats.

Please note:
the total preparation time for
this recipe is more than 1 hour.

Vanilla rhubarb with white chocolate ice cream

500g (17.6oz) rhubarb, cut into cubes • 2 vanilla pods, in halves • 100g (3.53oz) hazelnuts, coarsely chopped • 100g (3.53oz) sugar • 100g (3.53oz) white chocolate • 2 tbsp cream • 2 eggs, the egg yolk • 2 dl (7floz) cream, whisked into soft peaks

1   Mix the rhubarb with the vanilla pods, the hazelnuts and 80g (2.8oz) sugar. Leave for 1 hour.
2   Bring the mixture to the boil and let it simmer for 3 minutes, and then let it cool.
3   Melt the white chocolate in a bain-marie with the cream.
4   Whisk the egg yolk and the remaining sugar in a bain-marie till you have a smooth mixture. Whisk this mixture with ice till it becomes cold in a bain-marie.
5   Successively spoon in the melted chocolate and the cream. Freeze this mixture.
6   Serve the chocolate ice cream with the rhubarb mixture.

Please note:
the total preparation time for
this recipe is more than 5 hours.

Chocolate flan

1 small jar of cherries with syrup (350g (12.3oz) • 100g (3.53oz) sugar • 1.5dl (5.2floz) cream
• 1.5dl (5.2floz) Pedro Ximénez (sherry) • 100g (3.53oz) chocolate • 7 large egg yolks

1 Preheat the oven to 130°Celsius (250°Fahrenheit, Gas mark ½).
2 Drain the cherries in a sieve and collect the syrup.
3 Reduce the syrup with half of the sugar till there is only a little bit left in the bottom of the pan. Spoon the syrup and the cherries into the bottom of 4 oven-proof dishes (150ml (5.2floz) content).
4 Heat the cream with the sherry on low heat and melt the chocolate in this mixture.
5 Whisk the yolks with the remaining sugar till it is creamy. Add the warm chocolate mixture slowly.
6 Divide the flan batter over the flan moulds. Place the flan moulds in a bowl with warm water and put this in the preheated oven for 40 minutes.
7 Let the flans cool. Eat them straight out of the flan moulds or immerse them for a short time in hot water, then tip out onto a plate.

Liquid ginger-chocolate cake

3dl (10.5floz) milk • 75g (2.6oz) chocolate • ½ tsp vanilla-essence • 100g (3.53oz) icing sugar (or soft sugar) • 100g (3.53oz) butter • 150g (5.3oz) self-raising flour • 2 tbsp cocoa powder • 50g (1.76oz) stem ginger, chopped finely • **To make the sauce:** 3 tbsp cocoa powder • 50g (1.76oz) sugar • 2dl (7floz) water • 1dl (3.5floz) ginger syrup

1   Preheat the oven to 180° Celsius (350°Fahrenheit, Gas mark 4).
2   Warm the milk over a low heat. Melt the chocolate in the milk. Add the vanilla essence and take the pan off the heat.
3   Mix the icing sugar with the butter till it becomes creamy.
4   Mix the self-raising flour with the cocoa powder and stir this through the butter creme. Add this mixture and the stem ginger to the chocolate milk and stir till it becomes a smooth, liquid cake batter. Pour this cake batter into a round baking dish or cake mould.
5   Mix the cocoa powder together with the sugar to make the sauce. Heat the water and add a little to the cocoa. Stir well and then add the remaining water and ginger syrup.
6   Pour the chocolate sauce over the cake batter. Do not stir!
7   Bake the cake in the preheated oven. During baking, the cake will separate from the sauce. The result is an airy chocolate cake with a liquid ginger chocolate sauce underneath.

Truffles

For 30-40 truffles • 150g (5.3oz) butter at room temperature • 1dl (3.5floz) sugared, condensed milk • 250g (8.8oz) pure chocolate, melted • 300-500g (10.6-17.6oz) chocolate, at the correct tempering temperature • cocoa powder.

1   Mix the butter with the milk in a bowl.
2   Add the melted chocolate. Whisk everything well and then put the mixture in piping bag.
3   Form truffles on greaseproof paper and let them stiffen in the fridge.
4   Immerse the truffles in the blended chocolate and then roll them through the cocoa powder.

Chocolate muffins

60g (2.1oz) chocolate • 2 tbsp butter • 4 tbsp olive oil • 3 tbsp honey • 2 eggs • 2 tbsp cane sugar • 50g (1.76oz) flour • ½ tsp vanilla sugar • pinch of salt • 35g (1.25oz) walnuts, chopped

1   Preheat the oven to 160° Celsius (320° Fahrenheit, Gas mark 3).
2   Melt the chocolate over low heat together with the butter and olive oil.
3   Take the pan off the heat and mix the melted chocolate with the honey till it becomes a smooth mixture.
4   With the hand blender, whisk the eggs and the cane sugar till it is an airy mixture.
5   Mix the chocolate mixture with the whisked eggs and add the flour, vanilla sugar and salt.
6   Fill 8 muffin moulds with the mixture and divide the walnuts over them.
7   Bake the muffins for 20 minutes in a preheated oven.

White chocolate mousse
with passion fruit

2 egg whites • 1.5dl (5.2floz) cream • 500g (17.6oz) white sugar • 5dl (17.5floz) cream,
whisked into soft peaks • 4 passion fruits, the flesh

1   Whisk the egg whites. Heat the cream and melt the chocolate in it.
2   Let the mixture cool a little and mix in the cream.
3   Carefully spoon in the egg whites.
4   Portion the mousse into 4 glasses and let it stiffen for at least 4 hours in the fridge.
5   Take the glasses out of the fridge and divide the passion fruit over the mousse.

Please note:
the total preparation time for
this recipe is more than 4 hours.

Chocolate roll with lemon and banana

To make the cake dough: butter for greasing • 4 eggs • 100g (3.53oz) sugar • 100g (3.53oz) flour • 50g (1.76oz) cocoa powder • grated peel of ½ lemon • **To make the filling:** 2 bananas • juice of 1 lemon • 2dl (7floz) whipped cream • 75g (2.6oz) chocolate, in small pieces • 1 tbsp sugar

1   Preheat the oven to 170° Celsius (325° Fahrenheit, Gas mark 3).
2   Beat the eggs with the sugar and then whisk till foamy.
3   Sieve the flour and cocoa and mix this together with the whisked eggs. Add the lemon peel.
4   Divide the mixture over the baking tray (about 1cm, 0.4 inches thick) and bake for 7 minutes in the preheated oven.
5   Meanwhile make the filling; mash the banana with the lemon juice and mix in the cream and the pieces of chocolate.
6   Roll the warm cake in a damp cloth that has been sprinkled with sugar. Roll out the cake again and divide the filling over it.
7   Roll up the cake again (without cloth). Tuck the ends in and sprinkle the roll with sugar.

Sweet as Candy
For kids

Strawberry sandwich with mascarpone cream

6 slices of white bread with crust • 250g (8.8oz) strawberries, in slices
• **To make the mascarpone cream:** 250g (8.8oz) mascarpone • 100g (3.53oz) cream,
whisked into soft peaks • 4 tbsp icing sugar (or soft sugar)

1   Toast the bread in a toaster or under the grill. Cut one large and one small round out of each piece of toast.
2   Mix the mascarpone, the cream and the icing sugar together.
3   Spread the mascarpone cream onto the pieces of toast and put the slices of strawberry on them. Build a tower with 2 pieces of toast.

Crêpes with bilberries (blueberries)

75g (2.6oz) flour • 1 egg • 2dl (7floz) milk • 1 tbsp sugar • pinch of salt • butter • 200g (7oz) bilberries (blueberries)

1   Mix the flour, egg, milk, sugar and salt together and make a smooth batter.
2   Melt a knob of butter and stir this into the batter together with the bilberries (blueberries).
3   Repeatedly scoop small amounts of batter into a hot, greased frying pan with a spoon and make biscuits or crêpes.

TIP delicious with cream and a serving of ice cream.

Apple crumble

To make the filling: 4 apples, cut into small pieces • 1 tbsp cinnamon • 2 tbsp sugar • butter or oil for greasing • **To make the dough:** 75g (2.6oz) butter • 75g (2.6oz) sugar • 100g (3.53oz) flour or whole-wheat flour • 50g (1.76oz) oat flakes • pinch of salt • **To make the aniseed cream:** 2dl (7floz) cream • 2 tbsp ground aniseed sprinkles

1   Preheat the oven to 200° Celsius (400°Fahrenheit, Gas mark 6).
2   Mix the pieces of apple with the cinnamon and the sugar.
3   Portion the mixture into 4 small, greased baking dishes.
4   To make the dough, mix all the ingredients together till they become crumbly.
5   Sprinkle the crumble over the apples (do not press down) and put the dishes in the preheated oven for about 15 minutes.
6   Whisk the cream together with the aniseed sprinkles into stiff peaks.
7   Let the apple crumble cool a little and decorate with the aniseed cream.

Banana stracciatella

4-5 ripe bananas, peeled and cut into pieces • 1 tbsp lemon juice • 100g (5.3oz) icing sugar (or soft sugar) • 3dl (10.4floz) cream, whisked into soft peaks • 100g (5.3oz) almonds (or macadamia nuts) • 2 tbsp sugar • 100g (5.3oz) pure chocolate

1   Mix the pieces of banana with the lemon juice and the icing sugar in a mixer till the mixture becomes smooth.
    Add the cream that has been whisked into soft peaks.
2   Roast the almonds with the sugar, when cooled, chop finely.
3   Mix the chopped nuts and the pieces of chocolate into the banana mixture.
4   Put the mixture in the freezer for about two hours.

 Please note:
the total preparation time for
this recipe is more than 2 hours.

Cinnamon ice-cream cake

For 6-8 people • 6 tbsp cinnamon powder • 5 tbsp icing sugar • 500g (17.6oz) vanilla ice-cream • 2 small vanilla sticks, grated • 8 cinnamon flavoured sweets

1   Mix the cinnamon powder with the icing sugar in a small bowl.
2   Add 2 tablespoons water and stir till you have a smooth mixture.
3   Melt the ice and mix in the cinnamon mixture.
4   Take a round cake tin and line it with aluminium foil. Spoon in the beaten mixture and make it nice and smooth.
5   Cover the cake tin with a plate and put it in the freezer for 4 hours till it is frozen.
6   Take the ice out of the cake tin and put it on a flat plate. If you have any difficulty, hold the cake tin in hot water for a little while. Remove the foil.
7   Sprinkle the grated cinnamon over the ice-cream cake. Divide the cinnamon flavoured sweets over the cake.

Please note:
the total preparation time for
this recipe is more than 4 hours.

Vanilla ice-cream with toffees and marshmallows

1L (35floz) vanilla ice-cream • 150g (5.3oz) soft toffee • 200g (7oz) marshmallows

1   Put the ice-cream in the fridge for 2 hours to let it soften.
2   Cut 100g (3.53oz) toffees and 100g (3.53oz) marshmallows in small pieces and mix these through the soft ice-cream. Freeze the ice cream once more.
3   Serve the ice-cream with the remaining toffees and marshmallows.

Please note:
the total preparation time for
this recipe is more than 2 hours.

Wafer mille-feuille with pineapple

1dl (3.5floz) ginger syrup • 1dl (3.5floz) lemonade syrup • 1 pineapple, peeled and cut into thin slices • 250g (8.8oz) mascarpone • 1 tsp ginger root, grated • 1 pack of thin wafers

1 Mix the ginger syrup with the lemonade syrup and put the slices of pineapple in this mixture. Let them marinate for at least 30 minutes in the fridge.
2 Drain the slices of pineapple well and collect the pineapple juice.
3 Beat the mascarpone with the ginger root and 3 tablespoons pineapple juice till it you have a light mixture.
4 Scoop a spoonful of the mascarpone mixture onto a wafer and lay a few slices of pineapple on top.
5 Cover the pineapple with the mascarpone mixture and put a wafer on top.
6 Garnish with a little mascarpone and a piece of pineapple.

Orange sorbet

60ml (2floz) water • 1 tbsp grated orange rind • 150g (5.3oz) cane sugar • 7 oranges • juice of 1 lemon

1 Bring the water, orange rind and sugar to the boil, cook till the mixture becomes syrupy.
2 Cut the tops off 4 oranges and squeeze them out carefully. Clean the inside of the oranges as much as possible.
   Place them in the freezer.
3 Squeeze out the remaining oranges.
4 Add the lemon juice to the syrup and fill the oranges with the orange juice to 4dl (14floz).
5 Freeze the mixture for 8 hours and stir the ice around every two hours.
6 Fill the frozen oranges with the mixture.

Please note:
the total preparation time for
this recipe is more than **8 hours.**

Star apple lollies

8 nice star apples • 8 lolly sticks • butter for greasing • 1.5dl (5.2floz) syrup • 1.5dl (5.2floz) sugar •
150g (5.3oz) castor sugar • 1.5dl (5.2floz) cream • 1 tsp salt • 75ml (2.5floz) water • 3 tbsp butter

1   Take the stalks off the apples and replace them with lolly sticks.
2   Grease a piece of baking paper lightly with a little butter.
3   Put the syrup, all the sugar, the salt and the water in a pan with a thick bottom. Bring to the boil and keep stirring till it takes on a golden brown caramel colour. (Take care! The browning process can go very quickly. The sugar can turn black swiftly. Take the pan directly off the heat as soon as the sugar starts to go brown).
4   Beat the butter through the caramel when the pan has been taken off the heat.
5   While the caramel is still hot, work quickly; roll the apples through the mixture so they become evenly covered on all sides. Let the excess caramel flow back into the pan. Lay the apples on the baking paper to cool.

Strawberry mousse tartlet

1 small tray of strawberries • 150g (5.3oz) whole, the rest in pieces • 50ml (1.7floz) cottage cheese
• 1 egg yolk • 20g (0.7oz) icing sugar (or soft sugar) • 3 egg whites • 60g (2.1oz) sugar
• juice of ½ lemon • 3 sheets gelatin soaked in cold water • 1dl (3.5floz) cream, whisked into stiff peaks
• 1 pack of filo pastry • icing sugar

1   Purée 150g (5.3oz) of whole strawberries in the food processor or use the hand blender. Take 1dl (3.5floz) purée and mix this through the cottage cheese.
2   Whisk the egg yolk with the icing sugar till it becomes a light, foamy mixture.
3   Whisk the egg whites till they are very stiff and stir the sugar in gradually.
4   Bring the lemon juice to the boil. Squeeze out the gelatin and dissolve the sheets in the lemon juice.
5   Mix the whisked egg yolk with the cottage cheese mixture. Stir in the lemon juice, the egg whites, and finally the cream. Let the mousse stiffen for 4 hours.
6   Preheat the oven to 200° Celsius (400°Fahrenheit, Gas mark 6).
7   Cut 16 rounds out of the filo pastry. Bake the rounds for about 15 minutes in the preheated oven till they are brown and crispy. Sprinkle with icing sugar.
8   Divide the sheets of pastry onto 4 plates. Spread a generous helping of strawberry mousse on each sheet and put a few pieces of strawberry on top, then filo pastry again, mousse and strawberries and finally a sheet of pastry. Sprinkle ample icing sugar over the tartlets.

Please note:
the total preparation time for
this recipe is more than 4 hours.

Waffles

500g (17.6oz) flour • 6dl (20.5floz) milk • 50g (1.76oz) butter, melted • 2 eggs
• 2 tsp baking powder • pinch of salt • butter for greasing

1   Mix the butter and the milk together well till all lumps have gone (use a hand blender if necessary).
2   Add the melted butter, eggs and milk and mix well till you have a smooth batter with consistency of yogurt.
3   Bake the waffle in a preheated waffle iron. Grease the iron for each waffle with a brush with a little butter on it.
    Use 1dl (3.4floz) batter per waffle.

TIP serve the waffle with jam, icing sugar and/or creme fraiche.

Sweet Dreams
Desserts

Ricotta pudding with strawberries

250g (8.8oz) ricotta • 150g (5.3oz) mascarpone • 2 eggs, divided • juice of 2 lemons • 50g (1.76oz) sugar + 2 tbsp sugar • 250g (8.8oz) strawberries, cut into small pieces

1   Beat the mascarpone well together with the egg yolks, the lemon juice, and 50g (1.76oz) sugar.
2   Spoon the strawberries into the mixture.
3   Whisk the egg whites and the remaining sugar into stiff peaks. Spoon the egg white carefully through the ricotta mixture.
4   Portion the pudding into 4 dishes and put them in the fridge for an hour.
5   Garnish the puddings with whole strawberries just before serving.

Please note:
the total preparation time for
this recipe is more than 1 hour.

Thick yogurt with peaches and plums compote

1.5l (34floz) yogurt • 250g (8.8oz) blue plums, cut into small pieces • 100g (3.53oz) sugar
• 1 tsp lemon juice • 4-6 ripe peaches, peeled and in segments • sprigs of mint or lemon balm

1   Place a large round sieve above a bowl and line it with a clean, closely woven towel, for example a linen table napkin.
    Pour the yogurt onto the napkin and let it filter through for half a day.
2   Cook the plums with the sugar and the lemon juice till the plums are soft (about 10 minutes). Let them cool.
3   Divide the peaches over the high glasses. Pour the thick yogurt onto the peaches and divide the plum compote over it.
    Garnish with sprigs of mint or lemon balm.

TIP the thick yogurt and the compote can be made a day beforehand.

Please note:
the total preparation time for
this recipe is more than 12 hours.

Lime ice-cream with banana mousse

To make the ice-cream : 2dl (7floz) water • 350g (12.3oz) sugar • 80g (2.8oz) glucose syrup (or light corn syrup) • 5dl (17.2floz) lime juice • rind of 1 lime, grated • **To make the banana mousse:** 2 bananas • juice of ½ lemon • 2dl (7floz) cream • 2 tbsp sugar

1   To make the ice-cream, bring the water with the sugar and the syrup to the boil till all the sugar has dissolved and the syrup has a clear colour.
2   Take the pan off the heat and mix the contents with the lime juice. Add the grated lime peel and put the ice-cream mix-ture in the fridge for two hours till it has frosted over.
3   Put the ice cream in an ice cream maker.
4   Make the banana mousse just before serving as it becomes brown quickly. Purée 1½ bananas and the lemon juice with a hand blender. Keep half a banana for garnishing.
5   Whisk the cream and the sugar into stiff peaks and spoon it together with the cream through the puréed banana.
6   Portion the ice cream into coupes and serve it with the banana mousse. Garnish the ice cream with slices of banana and perhaps a slice of lime.

TIP if you not have an ice cream maker, buy ready-made lemon ice-cream.

Please note:
the total preparation time for
this recipe is more than 2 hours.

Mascarpone brûlée

4 egg yolks • 60g (2.1oz) sugar • 350g (12.3oz) mascarpone • 1dl (3.5floz) cream
• 1 tsp orange rind, grated • 50g (1.76oz) pure chocolate • 2 tbsp brown sugar

1   Preheat the oven to 150° (300° Fahrenheit, Gas mark 2).
2   Beat the egg yolks with the sugar into soft peaks.
3   Mix the mascarpone, cream and grated orange rind through the egg mixture.
4   Portion the mixture into 4 dishes and put them in a bowl of water in the preheated oven for 45 minutes
5   Let the dishes cool and mix the chocolate through the mascarpone mixture. Then let it cool a bit more.
6   Sprinkle the dishes with brown sugar and caramelize with a blow torch or under the grill.

 Please note:
the total preparation time for
this recipe is more than 1 hours.

Pear parfait

400g (14.1oz) tinned pears, drained (keep the syrup) • 4 egg yolks • 50g (1.76oz) sugar • 1.5dl (5.2floz) cream, whisked into stiff peaks • 2 tbsp pear liqueur • 1 pear, not peeled • icing sugar (or soft sugar)

1   Preheat the oven to 120° Celsius (248° Fahrenheit, Gas mark ½).
2   Purée the tinned pears in the food processor.
3   Whisk the egg yolks with sugar in a bain-marie till it becomes frothy. Take the mixture off the heat and keep whisking till it is cold.
4   Mix the cream through the mixture and then add the pear purée, 4 tablespoons pear syrup and the pear liqueur.
5   Spoon the mixture into forms of your choice and let the parfait stiffen in the fridge for 5 hours.
6   Cut the pear into very thin slices and dry them in the preheated oven.
7   Sprinkle the slices with icing sugar and serve with the parfait.

Please note:
the total preparation time for
this recipe is more than 5 hours.

Tartlet with spicy biscuits and cinnamon

2.5dl (8.5floz) milk • 1 cinnamon stick • 1 tsp mixed spices • 2 egg yolks • 50g (1.76oz) sugar • 4 sheets of gelatin, soaked in cold water • 2.5dl (8.5floz) cream, in soft peaks • **To make the sauce:** 4 egg yolks • 5 tbsp sugar • 2dl (7floz) apple cider • 2dl (7floz) white wine • 1 apple, peeled and cut into pieces • cinnamon powder

1 Heat the milk with the cinnamon stick and the mixed spices till it comes to the boil.
2 Whisk the egg yolks with the sugar till it becomes foamy. Stir in the milk mixture and warm everything up again but do not let it boil again. Keep stirring till it binds.
3 Dissolve the squeezed out gelatin in this mixture and sieve it. Let it cool a little and stir in the cream.
4 To make the sauce, beat the egg yolks with the sugar in a bowl till frothy. Place the bowl in a bain-marie and keep beating till the mixture becomes smooth and clear.
5 Heat the apple cider together with the wine and the apple for 1 minute. Let the mixture cool and whisk it through the egg mixture.
6 Divide the sauce over the tartlets and garnish them with a little cinnamon powder.

Please note:
the total preparation time for
this recipe is more than 4 hours.

Flan Catalan

To make the caramel: 4 tbsp sugar • 4 tbsp water • **To make the flan:** 375ml (12.9floz) milk
• 1 vanilla pod • 1 egg • 3 egg yolks • 100g (3.53oz) sugar

1   Preheat the oven to 200 Celsius° (400° Fahrenheit, Gas mark 6).
2   To make the caramel, heat the sugar and the water in 4 moulds by putting them in the preheated oven for 8 minutes or just on the cooker. When the sugar starts to colour a little, tilt the moulds in such a way that the inside becomes covered with the caramel. Put the moulds aside.
3   Then set the oven to 175° Celsius (350°Fahrenheit, Gas mark 4)
4   To make the flan, let the milk simmer with the vanilla pod for 15 minutes on low heat.
5   Whisk the egg, the egg yolks and the sugar. Add the warm milk gradually while stirring briskly.
6   Sieve the mixture and pour it into the caramel covered moulds.
7   Put the moulds in a high-sided baking dish in the preheated oven. Fill this with boiling water up to two thirds of the height of the moulds (If you put 2 or 3 egg shells in the water, the boiling water will not splash into the flans).
8   Have a look if the flans are ready after about 50 minutes. Use a satay stick to prick in the flans; it should come out clean.
9   Take the moulds out of the oven and let the flans cool. Tip the flans out onto a flat dish before serving (keep the moulds in hot water for a little while if they won't come out easily).

Please note:
the total preparation time for
this recipe is more than 1 hour.

Berry parfait

200g (7oz) bilberries (blueberries) • 100g (3.53oz) sugar • juice of 1 lime • 3 egg yolks • 3dl (10.3floz) cream, whisked into soft peaks

1   Bring the berries and 40g (1.4oz) sugar to the boil while stirring. Let the mixture cook for 5 minutes. Keep a few berries for garnishing.
2   Purée the berries with the hand blender or in a food processor.
3   Stir in the lime juice and rub the mixture through a fine sieve. Let the purée cool.
4   Whisk the remaining egg yolks and the rest of the sugar in a bain-marie till the mixture starts to bind. Take the pan off the heat and keep whisking till cold.
5   Fold first the berry purée and then the cream through the cooled egg mixture.
6   Spoon the mixture into a mould or into small moulds and put the parfait in the freezer for 12 hours. Finally, garnish with berries.

Please note:
the total preparation time for
this recipe is more than 12 hours.

Nectarines with raspberry sauce

For 2 people: 1 vanilla pod, cut open • 4 tbsp honey • 3 nectarines, seeded, peeled and halved • 75g (2.6oz) (deep-freeze) raspberries • 2 scoops of vanilla ice-cream • 50g (1.76oz) pure chocolate • pinch of nutmeg

1   Make the syrup by heating the vanilla pod slowly with the honey and a spoonful of water.
2   Poach the nectarines in the syrup till they are soft but do not fall apart. Drain and leave to cool.
3   Crush the (frozen) berries and mix with 4 tablespoons of the honey syrup. Let the mixture cool.
4   Portion the ice-cream into 2 coupes and put the poached nectarine halves on top of the ice-cream. Then add the grated chocolate and the nutmeg.

Plum tartlet with white chocolate sabayon

4 sheets of puff pastry • 60g (2.1oz) white chocolate • 2 egg yolks • 50g (1.76oz) flour
• 1 tsp baking powder • 2 tbsp water • 8 plums, cut into thin slices • **To make the sabayon:**
2 tbsp water • 2 tbsp sugar • 4 egg yolks • 30g (1oz) white chocolate • 70g (2.5oz) creme fraiche

1 Preheat the oven to 180° Celsius (350°Fahrenheit, Gas mark 4).
2 Roll the sheets of puff pastry out thinly and cut 3 small rounds of 5 to 7cm (2 to 2.75inches) from each sheet.
3 Melt the white chocolate in a bain-marie and add the egg yolks. Take the pan off the heat.
4 Sieve the flour with the baking powder and stir in the white chocolate mixture. Add the water to make
   a spreadable batter.
5 Spread the batter on the puff pastry rounds then make 4 stacks each with 3 of these rounds.
6 Lay the slices of plum in a fan shape on top of the stacks and bake these for 25 minutes in a preheated oven.
7 Make the sabayon just before serving the tartlets; whisk the water, the sugar and the egg yolks with a hand blender in a
   bain-marie till the mixture becomes airy. Add the chocolate as soon as the egg yolks begin to stiffen. Take the pan off the
   heat, stir the creme fraiche well and add to the sabayon.
8 Serve the plum tartlets with the chocolate sabayon.

Schwarzwald cake and kirsch in a glass

30g (1oz) cocoa • 75g (2.6oz) flour • 75g (2.6oz) cornflour (cornstarch) • 5 eggs • 150g (5.3oz) sugar • rind of 1 lemon, grated • butter or oil for greasing • 2 tbsp kirsch • 5dl (17.3floz) cream • 100g (3.53oz) sugar • 1 jar of cherries without stones, drained • extra flour for dusting

1   Preheat the oven to 200 Celsius° (400° Fahrenheit, Gas mark 6).
2   Stir the cocoa, the flour and the cornflour together well.
3   Mix the eggs, sugar and lemon peel well. Whisk this mixture in a bain-marie till it binds.
4   Take the egg mixture off the heat and whisk till it has cooled and become nice and airy.
5   Fold in the cocoa mixture. Grease a cake tin that is 3cm (1.1inches) high with butter and dust it with flour. Spoon the batter in and bake for 25 minutes in a preheated oven.
7   Cut rounds out of the dough with a cutting ring or knife and sprinkle these with the kirsch.
8   Whisk the cream and the sugar into stiff peaks.
9   Put a round piece of cake into each of the 4 glasses. Spoon the cherries and cream of top and cover this with another layer of cake. Repeat this till the glass is full.

Caramelized pineapple with vanilla parfait

1 pineapple, peeled and cut into 4 slices of 2cm (0.75in) • 50g (1.76oz) sugar
• **To make the vanilla parfait:** 3 egg yolks • 140g (5oz) sugar • 1 sachet vanilla sugar
• 3 egg whites • 4dl (13.8floz) cream, whisked into soft peaks • **To make the caramel frame:**
1 tbsp water • 2 tbsp sugar • 2 tbsp glucose syrup

1   To make the vanilla parfait, whisk the egg yolks with half of the sugar in a bowl in a bain-marie.
2   Fill a larger bowl or the sink with cold water, put the bowl in it and whisk till the mixture is cold.
3   Whisk the egg whites into stiff peaks with the remaining sugar.
4   Spoon the cream and the egg whites through the egg yolk mixture. Spoon it into a cake tin and put this in the freezer for at least 5 hours.
5   Make the caramel frames in the meantime. Bring the water slowly to the boil with the sugar and glucose.
6   Take the pan off the heat when the mixture starts to colour and let if cool off a little.
7   Put a piece of baking paper on the work space. Take a spoonful of sugar syrup and make, with a rotating movement, the form that you want. If the sugar becomes too hard, warm it up again.
8   Prepare the pineapple just before serving. Put it in a hot frying pan and sprinkle half the amount of sugar over it.
9   Let the pineapple brown a little (caramelize). Turn the slices over and sprinkle the remaining sugar over them. Let the slices brown again. Spoon the parfait onto the slices of pineapple and garnish with a caramel frame.

Please note:
the total preparation time for
this recipe is more than 5 hours.

Strawberry tiramisu

3 eggs, divided • 75g (2.6oz) sugar • 1 sachet vanilla sugar • 250g (8.8oz) mascarpone
• 50ml (1.7floz) espresso • 1tbsp forest fruit liqueur or crème de cassis • 16 sponge fingers
• 250g (8.9oz) strawberries

1 Whisk the egg yolks with the sugar and the vanilla sugar till it becomes a thick, yellowish cream.
2 Whisk the egg whites into stiff peaks.
3 Spoon the mascarpone through the egg yolk cream and then carefully fold in the egg white.
4 Mix the espresso with the fruit liqueur. Place half the sponge fingers in a suitable dish and sprinkle half the coffee mixture over them.
5 Divide half the strawberries over the sponge fingers and spoon the mascarpone mixture over them. Make another layer with the remaining sponge fingers and strawberries.
6 Cover the dish with plastic film and place in the fridge for at least 4 hours.

Please note:
the total preparation time for
this recipe is more than 4 hours.

Cinnamon parfait with baked apple

1 tbsp sugar • 2 tbsp honey • 1 tbsp lemon juice • 2 apples, peeled and cut into quarters
• 2dl (7floz) cream, whisked to the thickness of yogurt • 3 tbsp ginger syrup • cocoa powder
• **To make the parfait:** 200g (7oz) sugar • 2dl (7floz) water • 3 cinnamon sticks
• 8 egg yolks • 5dl (17.3floz) cream • tsp cinnamon, grated

1 To make the parfait, let the sugar and water simmer for half an hour with the cinnamon sticks.
2 Whisk the egg yolks with a hand blender till they become airy. Then carry on with whisking in a bain-marie till the egg yolks become stiff.
3 Take the cinnamon sticks out of the syrup and then pour it slowly into the egg yolks. Keep stirring. Take the pan off the heat and let the mixture cool to room temperature.
4 Beat the cream with the cinnamon powder till it is semi-solid and then mix it together with the egg yolk mixture.
5 Line a 1l (34floz) cake tin with baking paper or plastic film and pour the parfait into it. Let the parfait freeze for 8 hours.
6 Preheat the oven to 200 Celsius° (400° Fahrenheit, Gas mark 6).
7 Mix the sugar with the honey and the lemon juice and spread this over the quarters of apple. Put them on a baking tray and bake for 15 minutes in the preheated oven till nice and brown.
8 Mix the whisked cream with the ginger syrup.
9 Hold the cake tin under the hot tap and take the parfait out with the help of the baking paper. Cut the parfait in slices and serve with the baked apple and the ginger cream. Garnish with a little cocoa powder.

Please note:
the total preparation time for
this recipe is more than **8 hours.**

Raspberry soup

600g (21oz) raspberries • 50g (1.76oz) sugar • 2 tbsp strawberry liqueur • 125ml (4.3floz) creme fraiche • ½ tsp coriander (cilantro) powder

1 Put 100g (3.53oz) raspberries aside. Cook the remaining raspberries with the sugar on low heat.
2 Purée the raspberries with the liqueur and let this mixture cool.
3 Portion the purée into 4 small bowls and place the raspberries that were put aside into the mixture.
4 Whisk the creme fraiche with the coriander powder and put a spoonful in the soup.

Pistachio chocolate cake

For 8 people • **To make the cake base:** 100g (3.53oz) pistachio nuts, chopped
• 50g (1.76oz) butter, melted • 50g (1.76oz) castor sugar • 3 tbsp self-raising flour • 1 tsp orange juice
• **To make the filling:** 200g (7oz) white chocolate • 80ml (2.75floz) cream • 10g (0.4oz) butter
• 150ml (5.2floz) creme fraiche, whisked into soft peaks • 2 tbsp lemon juice • **For garnishing:**
100g (3.53oz) raspberries • 50g (1.76oz) chocolate flakes

1   Preheat the oven to 175° Celsius (350°Fahrenheit, Gas mark 4).
2   Mix the pistachio nuts, the butter, the castor sugar, the flour and the orange juice into a firm mixture. Let the cake dough rest for 30 minutes in the fridge and then press into a small cake tin. Bake it for 15 minutes in the oven and then let the cake base cool.
3   Melt the white chocolate together with cream and the butter. Mix the mixture with the hand blender till it is airy. Mix the creme fraiche and spoon in the orange juice.
4   Spread this mixture out onto the cooled cake base and let it stiffen over night.
5   Garnish with chocolate flakes and raspberries.

TIP serve with a scoop of raspberry ice-cream.

Sherry sorbet

200g (7oz) sugar • 6dl (20.5floz) water • 2.5dl (8.6floz) sherry (amontillado) • handful raisins, soaked in sherry

1 Heat the sugar till it turns brown.
2 Add 2dl (7floz) water and cook till it becomes syrupy. Let it cool.
3 Mix the sherry with the rest of the water and the syrup. Spin this mixture in an ice-cream maker till it becomes a sorbet and put the mixture in the freezer for 4 hours. Tap it loose every half hour to prevent ice crystals forming.
4 Serve the sorbet with the raisins.

Please note:
the total preparation time for
this recipe is more than 4 hours.

Citrus crumble with dates

To make the filling: I grapefruit, in segments • I orange in segments • I blood orange in segments • 2 tangerines, in segments • 220g (7.8oz) sugar • 2.5dl (8.7floz) water • 8 dates, in small pieces • I tsp freshly ground black pepper • **To make the crumble:** • 100g (3.53oz) cold butter, in small pieces • 100g (3.53oz) cane sugar • 160g (5.6oz) flour • butter for greasing

I   Take the skin off the segments of the citrus fruits. Place them tightly together in a pan.
2   Add sugar and water and lay a heat resistant plate on the fruit. Simmer for I hour in this way.
3   Subsequently, let the fruit cool in a sieve for at least I hour.
4   Spoon the dates and the black pepper carefully through the fruit.
5   Preheat the oven to 225°Celsius (437°Fahrenheit, Gas mark 7).
6   To make the crumble, mix the butter, cane sugar and flour into a crumbly, sandy mixture.
7   Grease a baking dish with a diameter of about 22cm (8.6inches) with butter. Cover the bottom with fruit and divide the crumbly dough over it.
8   Put the dish in the preheated oven for 30 minutes. The crumble is ready when it has become golden brown.
9   Serve the citrus crumble in the baking tin, preferably when it is still justwarm.

Please note:
the total preparation time for
this recipe is more than 2,5 hours.

Cherry sorbet with cherry compote

750g (26.5oz) fresh cherries, without stones • 1 tbsp lemon juice • 250g (8.8oz) sugar
• 2dl (7floz) water • **To make the cherry compote:** 500g (17.6oz) fresh cherries, without stones,
chopped coarsely • 2 tbsp cherry liqueur • 1 tbsp lemonade syrup • 2 tbsp honey • 1 tbsp mint, cut finely

1 Purée the cherries with the lemon juice, the sugar and water. Spin the mixture in an ice-cream maker till it becomes
   a sorbet.
2 To make the cherry compote, mix the cherries with the liqueur, lemonade syrup, honey and mint leaves. Cook this for
   5 minutes and then whisk till it becomes a coarse mixture. Let it cool.
3 Fill a high glass with a spoonful of cherry compote and add a scoop of sorbet.

Smooth & Sweet
Drinks

Cranberry apple smoothie

2 stalks of blanched celery • 2 apples • 100g (3.53oz) cranberries • 2cm (0.75 inches) ginger • a little mint

Crush all the ingredients in a liquidizer (juicer) and add 2 ice cubes. Garnish with a few cranberries.

Chocolate split

1 dl (3.4floz) chocolate sauce • 2 bananas • 1 tbsp. cocoa powder • 2.5 dl (8.5floz) vanilla ice cream • 2.5 dl (8.5floz) milk

Mix all the ingredients in the blender and serve cold.

Raspberry granita

100g (3.53oz) sugar • 1.5dl (5.2floz) water • juice of 1 lemon • 200g (7oz) raspberries • 1 bottle cherry beer (if so desired)

1   Bring the sugar with the water and the lemon juice to the boil and stir the mixture till it becomes a syrup.
2   Wash the raspberries carefully and cook them, with the water that is still clinging to them, for 2 minutes.
3   Press the raspberries through a sieve and mix them with the syrup. Add the cherry beer if so desired.
4   Pour the raspberry mixture into a large, flat dish and cover this with cling film.
5   place the dish in thefreezer. After 2 hours stir the mixture with a fork to loosen it. Do this every hour, till all the liquid has frozen after about 6 hours.
6   Spoon the granita into glasses.

Please note:
the total preparation time for
this recipe is more than 6 hours.

Slush puppy with strawberries

To make 4 glasses: 500g (17.6oz) strawberries (freeze if necessary) • 3dl (10.3floz) mineral water, still (non-carbonated) • 4 tbsp strawberry syrup • 16 ice cubes crushed

1   Mix the strawberries with the water and syrup in a blender.
2   Portion the crushed ice into 4 glasses and pour the strawberry mixture on top.
3   Stir briefly and serve immediately.

Thai tango

To make 1 glass • 100g (3.53oz) fresh papaya, cut into slices • juice of 1 lime • 2 medium-sized pears, peeled and cut into slices • 2dl (7floz) rice milk • pinch of ground ginger

1   Mix all the ingredients
2   Pour the drink into a glass. Add ice cubes if so desired.

San Francisco smoothie

100g (3.53oz) strawberries, cut into pieces • 100g (3.53oz) fresh pineapple, cut into pieces • 1 dl (3.5floz) ice cold orange juice

1   Freeze the pieces of strawberry and pineapple for at least 1 hour in the freezer.
2   Purée the strawberries, the pineapple and the orange juice in a food processor or with a hand blender. Pour the mixture into a high glass and serve cold.

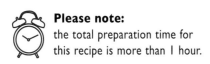

Please note:
the total preparation time for
this recipe is more than 1 hour.

Index